T0161235

CLINCH

CLiNCH

Selected Poems
by Michael Scholnick

Edited by Gary Lenhart,

Steve Levine,

Greg Masters,

and Bob Rosenthal

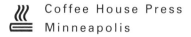
Coffee House Press
Minneapolis

ACKNOWLEDGMENTS

Some of these poems appeared in *Chelys, Mag City, mini, New Directions #37, Poetry Project Newsletter, Tangerine, United Artists,* and *The World.* We thank the editors of those publications and apologize to those we have overlooked. Much thanks to Robert Creeley, Chris Edgar, Anselm Hollo, Michael Kellner, Elizabeth Murray, Eileen Myles, Alice Notley, Ron Padgett, and the Paula Cooper Gallery, and to Nellie Scholnick.

Coffee House Press is supported in part by a grant provided by the Minnesota State Arts Board, through an appropriation by the Minnesota State Legislature, and in part by a grant from the National Endowment for the Arts. Significant support has also been provided by the McKnight Foundation; Lannan Foundation; Jerome Foundation; Target Stores, Dayton's, and Mervyn's by the Dayton Hudson Foundation; General Mills Foundation; The St. Paul Companies; Butler Family Foundation; Honeywell Foundation; Star Tribune/Cowles Media Company; James R. Thorpe Foundation; Dain Bosworth Foundation; Pentair, Inc.; Beverly J. and John A. Rollwagen Fund of the Minneapolis Foundation; the Peter & Madeleine Martin Foundation; the law firm of Schwegman, Lundberg, Woessner & Kluth, P.A.; and many individual donors. To you and our many readers across the country, we send our thanks for your continuing support.

Coffee House Press books are available to the trade through our primary distributor, Consortium Book Sales & Distribution, 1045 Westgate Drive, Saint Paul, MN 55114. For personal orders, catalogs, or other information, write to: Coffee House Press, 27 N. 4th Street, Suite 400, Minneapolis, MN 55401.

LIBRARY OF CONGRESS CATALOGING-IN-PUBLICATION DATA
Scholnick, Michael.
    Clinch / Michael Scholnick : edited by Gary Lenhart . . . [et al.].
        p.   cm.
    ISBN 1-56689-070-5 (PB : ALK. PAPER)
    1. City and town life—New York (State)—New York—Poetry.
    2. Family—New York (State)—New York—Poetry.   I. Lenhart, Gary.
    II. Title.
    PS3569.C52544C57 1998
    811´.54—dc21   97-43269
                                                                    CIP

10   9   8   7   6   5   4   3   2   1

CONTENTS

PREFACE

Living in a war zone
Where we shine our badness to God.
My quick prayer:
Let the lamb lie down on Astor Pl.

A poet's poems stand as our best memory of him. *Clinch*
clinches it for Michael Scholnick. The poet arrived in
downtown New York City in 1975, part of the same cultural
bombardment as Patti Smith, the Nuyorican Poets Café,
and the last pure bohemian moment east of Second
Avenue. Bracketed by his timely arrival and elusive death,
his selected poems represent fifteen years of dazzling
work—poems alternately rich, sinewy, chiding, dense,
Yiddish, and sexy: "Friday come fast/Delicious word."

Even when he dabbled in traditional forms, Scholnick is
persistently revealed as a poet of single-line pileups and an
unconcealable lightness that makes you want to weep and
eat. "Life not enjoyed/To the utmost is a sin." Now *Clinch*
introduces Scholnick to a wider public that has only antic-
ipated him through his amalgam of influences. I think of
Notley, Charles Bernstein and Reznikoff, Amiri Baraka,
Gary Snyder, and Lorca. I envy the new readers of these
oddly declamatory poems of turgidity and sweetness.

An immobile will somehow
Of snow has fallen
Suspended on branches and clothesline

It's like watching a river rip through someone's soul, the
mud parts and it's a street. They read like New York.

—Eileen Myles

INTRODUCTION

Michael always made surprising and unusual perceptions and connections. He'd say something that could spark, jolt you, make you blink. Those perceptions were so different I felt he was connected to some other world, not like left field, but really a higher spiritual sphere.

—Rochelle Kraut

I always thought of Michael as chiseling his words out of the granite of experience and observation. He sculpted his poems into new forms of matter that rearranged images and responses into a startling new way of seeing and responding.

—Greg Masters

I used to think that Michael had an abstract arrangement to his mind. I thought him unhurried and excessively dreamy. As I listened more to Michael's speech, I heard that the long pauses punctuating phrase endings were carefully considered turns and that his odd timing was as original and melodious as Thelonious Monk's.

—Bob Rosenthal

Michael Scholnick was born in Queens, New York, in 1953 and grew up in the Bronx. He played third base and catcher in Little League baseball and, as he was fond of recounting, traveled to Puerto Rico on an all-star team. While in high school, he moved to Wilkes-Barre, Pennsylvania, with his ailing father. He attended Wilkes College and edited the student magazine, *Manuscript.* The highlight of his time at Wilkes came when he invited Gregory Corso to campus for a reading, after which Michael and Gregory went bowling. In 1973 he transferred to Rutgers University, where he received a B.A. degree in 1975. While an undergraduate at Rutgers, he participated in a poetry reading in the basement of the Corner Tavern; among the other readers were Miguel Algarin, Marilyn Kallet, and Nathaniel Tarn. In separate attendance and hearing him read for the first time were Greg Masters and Gary Lenhart, with whom he would edit the little magazine *Maq City* from 1977 to 1986.

After graduating from Rutgers, Michael moved to New York City's Lower East Side; he was to reside there for the rest of his life. During the next few years, he was in attendance regularly at the Poetry Project at St. Mark's Church and at the Nuyorican Poets Café. In 1976 he spent the summer studying poetics at Naropa Institute; he was a teaching assistant to Allen Ginsberg. In 1978 he was one of ten young men to have poems included in "Ginsberg's Choice" in *New Directions #37.* In an introduction to the poems, Ginsberg praised Michael's "beat optimist élan." That same year his first collection of poems, *Perfume,* was published by Steve Levine's Remember I Did This for You imprint.

In 1978 to 1980 he was employed by the United Jewish Council, working with elderly residents of the Lower East Side. From 1979 to 1981, under the federal government's CETA Title VII program, he worked with senior citizens through Teachers & Writers Collaborative, organized a series of poetry readings at the Snug Harbor Cultural Center on Staten Island, and, with poet Ravi Singh, organized the highly successful Poetry on Film, a series of film documentaries about poets, screened at Millennium Film Workshop.

In 1980 Michael received a Fellowship in Poetry from the National Endowment for the Arts. That same year his second chapbook of poems, *Beyond Venus,* was published by Crony Books. He also published two books of poems written collaboratively with Tom Weigel: *A Hot Little Number* and *Nations and Peace*. He remained active as an editor of *Mag City*, and he began to publish books by other poets under the Misty Terrace Press imprint. Among the poetry published by Misty Terrace were books by Cliff Fyman and Elinor Nauen, and a book of collaborations by James Schuyler and Helena Hughes.

Michael's first play, *Providence*, was performed at the Poetry Project as part of Bob Holman's Poets' Theatre Workshop in 1978. With Bob Rosenthal and Eileen Myles, he organized the Ear of the Dog Poets' Theatre Festival at Charas in 1982, where his second play, *Pay Day*, was produced. He continued to act in other Poets' Theatre productions, such as The Eye and Ear Theater's production of W.H. Auden's *Paid on Both Sides*.

In 1982 Michael and Nellie Villegas married. He began teaching in the New York City public school system, first at J.H.S. 60 in Manhattan and then at the Bronx High School of Science. He helped plan the experimental Mastery Learning Program in School District 1, which received a Recognition Award from the U.S. Department of Education in 1989. In spite of his teaching schedule, he continued to write poems, plays, book reviews, and art criticism at an impressive rate. In 1987 he wrote the catalog essay for Alex Katz's exhibition of paintings at the Robert Miller Gallery, "Alex Katz from the Early 60s." He wrote a four-act play, *You Got to Understand Something*, and assembled two manuscripts of poems, *Heart Melodies* and *Glancing at My Life*. Michael also enrolled in the Graduate School at New York University to study English and American literature. While studying American poetry with Harold Bloom, he wrote the critical appreciation, "Shaking Hands with James Schuyler."

In February 1989 a daughter, Elizabeth Meryl, was born to Nellie and Michael. Michael was devoted to his family and found great joy in spending time with his daughter. He had received his M.A. degree and was pleased with his new teaching position at Bronx Science. In early November 1990 he suffered an apparent heart stop and died suddenly.

At the memorial service for Michael held at the Poetry Project at St. Mark's Church, speakers consistently emphasized the spiritual and ethical aspects of Michael's character and work. All agreed that Michael was "a person of the highest integrity." His poems have something of the Hebrew prophets about them ("I soar, I continuously rage"). Michael was devoted to and inspired by the words of Yeats, Shelley, Moses Maimonides, and Charles Reznikoff. He took the most outrageous visionary claims with utmost seriousness, just as anyone with his abounding modesty, integrity, and genius would.

But if those who loved him concur that he possessed outstanding ethical and spiritual qualities, those who love his poems recognize that he was more complicated and playful than that implies. Michael had a wickedly impish wit that found amusement in odd corners of experience. His imagination made leaps as startling as those of an exuberant dancer. One often held one's breath until the leap was completed, awed by its sheer extravagance and made somewhat uncomfortable by the risk involved in the attempt. However righteous he might at times seem, Michael's imagination was primarily aesthetic. His poetry is perhaps best characterized by its extreme refinement, a quality not to be confused with manners or conventions. Michael's genius was abrupt and extraordinary, like an angel stepping onto a bus. He aimed at elegance and sometimes achieved it, but it is an elegance without facility. Michael had an innate dislike of the easy, even when it made things easier for everyone.

Marianne Moore wrote, "The poet commits himself to that one integrity: antipathy to falsity." Michael's poems demand readers deal with them in the uncompromising spirit in which they were composed. Michael thought the worst thing you could say of a poem was that it was "typical." His poems are not typical of anything, but are fresh, as he was, in every sense of the word. Michael's gifts were rare and mysterious. As his friends, we are going to miss him. As readers, we are grateful to Coffee House Press for publishing this book, which was compiled from four manuscripts (*Perfume, Beyond Venus, Glancing at My Life,* and *Heart Melodies*—the last two were unpublished) and from scattered magazine publications.

—The Editors

To
Nellie and Elizabeth Meryl Scholnick

HEROISM

You chuckle alone throat beats
Blood that intensifies emptiness
Day as well wheels a hammer cleat
Spiked something moodless

Sure tramps walk gaining by
All the same you recognize a coat
What unknown territory is priestly
Germane vision your head promotes

Aloud engine in a shack
There's quiche in spotless heaven
And sack to trade and plenty of Gaelic
Though bodiless uneven

Death from Time and Love a sheet separate
Like you loosely wrapped nothing to do with it

CATSKILL SONG AND DANCE

When Hank Williams sings
      "Like a piece of driftwood on the sea
      May you never be alone like me"
I don't compare him to Shakespeare
I say "that's beautiful"
and play it again

What's in store for America?
Higher prices? Years of my poetry?
A renaissance of pretense and fascism?
The scholarship of shadows?
Love syndicated and blest
as uninspired businessmen consume the nation tolerating words?

I'm so glad to learn what spirit is
Now I'm not hungry
I'm a disciple peeling an orange
I'm he who sits on steps
watching the rain fall
wishing to feel relieved
After a while I'm back inside
thinking the same old thoughts

Solitary as a Russian novel
I hang my head in sorrow

Sorrow? I can't finish with sorrow
Not after Frank O'Hara
His selected self collected in my kitchen
Fast? Man he was fast
He was so fast he's dead
He was faster than a day or a shower
Faster than the Middle Ages and faster

At work
No one wants to take out the garbage
The waitresses just won't do it
and are allowed not to
They yell "Garbage" when the bag is full
And someone
Could be me
Steps out front

And when I step out the back door
And toss the dripping goods over the black rail
Into the green bin perfect!
I look around
And sometimes I can see the moon

FOR IRWIN HEILNER

Experience is disappointing,
that's why life's absurd.
I learned this watching you shave
lecturing about Beethoven
and prison reform
Polite man bathrobed
standing in your living room
I was company
" . . . and all we can do," you said,
finger scanning skin neck cheeks
feeling baby red smooth skin,
"Is punish, punish, punish."
Now finding a hair then clipping
delicately
with a conductor's wrist

Wisdom flows in your speech
of an art to consciousness
heavier than Beethoven's fist
Amazing how he tamed such wildness
ordering blue soldiers in blue chariots
to march around the white Chinese teacup of his mind
How zapped with power he lifted his wrath
above the birds and clouds
above Napoleon's imagination
And smashed antiquity
dropping Quartets 14 15 & 16
on God's porcelain tongue

For you a musician
An eccentric librarian
whose deepest thoughts
dwell dusty and unpublished
The eternal is fierce and now
Who can deny your chilly chords?
For you scores of inspiration
Manuals cartons of sage sense
A humble universe
The science of your soul
in an unknown basement
on Dawson Avenue
in Clifton, New Jersey

FIELD TRIP

words are international energy
yours take off like a menu of everything
an aura unraveling my horrid scope
into a straight dialogue line
the architecture is serene
the german tourists have a road map and a camera
see that column no windows pure mass in the breeze
is it an american camera you ask
discarding observation for fact
though you don't speak german
you've been to france
and can recognize a good picture
over someone's shoulder when you see it
i have to go traveling you're right
so we leave the u.n. plaza
its blazing green swarm
bowling my thoughts into the east river
i have to get sunglasses you say
and disappear like a cigarette

AVENUE A

Noon morning walk
Pause at entrance
Iodine baby tears
Activate black dairy air
While Thank You Mary bells
Toll
I turn left
And a man crosses himself
Crammed fervent pilgrimage
770 Eastern Parkway
Judaism contained in a rebbe
What's he written? asks Jim
I want to see his hands
Say I am American amiable
Concerned with the American Idiom
Sturdy and detached
To quote Jamie MacInnis
Ask blessings for my father's soul
Depart death's master
Holy and human as love
"Ear stones" emit a neighborhood bright
Pentecostal wrists jingle
Spirits of the bandy-legged poor

LET IT GO

Let mayhem level fine weather
Let the ancient cortex dismount
Let pain lash and fructify
Tires slash and berate
Descendant roofs' southeastern view mottled

Let volcanoes interrupt favors
Wheels turbine wagon roar acrimonious
For points of view are rigid tasks
Saturn is desired, defective cloud ferns

For every minute has a rosy outlook
For molars like torsos hang in detail
For dependence is a virtue like spells of confusion
For Justice wins

Let cross-cultural righteousness style
Casual gladiolas in sink

MIDNIGHT

Darkness is a fine thing
Let us stay, and be lost.
True, it is inhuman, but
So is the summery sun.

ADDITION

Decorous barnward mist prevails
I, awe-struck, equestrian stare
And squeal, getting wood

AT NINTH CIRCLE

I don't mind this waiting for Love

Nude Publisher Carl
rich partner talk $100 sessions
grass smoked in blow-heated terrace

Sweet Al from Kentucky glows
shipping canvases to Georgia
Rothko switched to colors

grown suspicious in crowds
I left before 12

Reason sighs
For want of Grace

The heart, a woman's heart,
resplendent and mercurial,
inconstantly babbles

MY LADY IS LOVELY

The sky is her lamp
Horizon attached
A dilemma of relativity.
Sleep, my love

Laundry, butcher,
Supermarket, service.
The street hasn't a plan.

Convicts wig verisimilitude,
Hiding in tunnels, forging
Ladders, assuming a destiny.

Sleep, my love

Bets, stands, bunks, for sale.
Bialys, confections, fumes bake.
Her lips are Thailands.
Her thighs do rock.

Splash of ebullient puddle.
Clam arenas shade.
Dote meticulous alterations.

Chair embraces ground,
Thy tone consequent
Verges on mania.
One has to awake when one must.
Eavesdrop, sleep, my love, my love.

LUCILLE'S LOVE

Continued intrigue
thrown for a loop
Cocksucking passersby
Slothful meander fend

Midnight on the bay
The swishing is archaic
In the distance snuggle
Against a divine thought
Selfishness
          that borrower
Chucks inspiration

Persist in surrendering
A base person is a paradox
Om is boundless
Unclear blown-up
Colloquial antidepressant
Look on the lime remover truck

You called for a nuclear poem
Like a witch to hazel
Fury
     She had no father
Sickness Madness Beauty
A rolodex of Visions

No particular audit
Triumphing
Incredible substitution folly
The idyllic Tribe of Man

THE QUESTION

Her brother pursued
Nightclub circuits off-hours, stoic on piano,
Wrote oriented numbers, owned a van

She composed less commercially and
Sang like a ballplayer's retired uniform
I mean she learned a range
Beyond the normal amble
Her hair was rich, earth sloping
Like a deer's coat,
And thick and pure white

Early on, afraid of chaos
We covered one page with words
Shifting the letters in her name around
Urgently we lived together
And I went out west alone

Women she loved confused her,
Author of self's bliss, wanted their friendship
And eccentric caresses; creating art
Characters have breakdowns

It was the kind of family
That disagreed about method acting
While it snowed on
It's possible her mother
Willed our violent separation

GREG'S MUSIC

One's actions are inimitable.
Reflections contingent upon questions
Effect repose. The stove is clean.

Shaking in rooms, discontent
His fleet of opinion focuses.
In the unforseeable mandolin
He secures an ally.

Presently, the brave day is slaughtered.
The crisis disappears.

Our hero reads, relaxes,
Gains supremacy over alternatives
That resemble dreadful combat.
A margin of wine plays host.

I am used to strength.
Its language, a poem, my salvation's corollary.
Now crickets in the friendly weather
Bark in the radiation after dinner.

GOOD GRACES

I have no questions, Kiss me
Beggar's loving qualities
& branches, snow-pursued, Kiss me

Air of great, saber-toothed waves, Kiss me
Kiss me, instill something hilarious

Your step a nocturnal detail
Pregnant wind, remote & sketched
Centipede upon a balustrade of bedimmed sequence
Darkness of the woods' closure

Kiss me, I'm a gardener
No pills, Kiss me
I know I never doubted you
Teach me to drive

Light breaks through the blinds
The bird chirps inventing pleasure
I half-smiled at the bridge, Kiss me

Programs Tickets, Kiss me
Six dancers Two beats
See you soon, Good-night, Kiss me
Mixed reviews & Hula Hoops, Kiss me

Last call, Kiss me
Let's cut here, Kiss me
Sounds interesting, Kiss me
Alternative to coffee, Kiss me
One wish granted, Kiss me

Nervous rendezvous & seamy aftermath
Utterly heartless, amusement
Ignorance analogized
Diaphanous commonplace

You are scrubbed & absurd
In the wings of melancholy paroxysms, Kiss me
At a party with security guards, Kiss me

SPONTANEOUS POEM
FOR A CHILD'S NAME (ISAAC)

The door is open.
The hurricane spun into the sea.

There is much laughter everywhere,
In the circuits of the wind.

I think, like the wind,
I shall inwardly exult, too.

Last night, while the sun laughed,
The great rain continued.

Ah, management approves of my task.

I am inconspicuous.
I think with the sun
I shall laugh, endlessly.

NEW JOB POEMS

1.

Actually,
their lives are bare.
Nature's astonished them.

Inspired Meltzer raves:
I lost my name.

Bright brown his dog
tugs on a string.

2.

I'd rather live
with Gypsies, rats & colored people
than in city housing.

That's Philosophy, Geography & History.
Morris Fluxgold.

I'd rather be dead in Spain.
Fanatics. Gangsters. Bastards.

I'm not from Mars, I tell him.

They chased me 100 blocks
when my parents died, for what?

3.

Lutheran Church Neighborhood
Garden 9th & A

   Anyone caught
  on these premises
 will be punished
   to the fullest extent. This means
      death.

    +

  God Bless You

& Ease
The Will of the people

4.

Celia Rosenbaum, taught High Schul.
Torah. Writing. Prophets.

It happens that I like music. Opera also.
I once told a musician,
  "Music is the climate of my soul."
He said I was philosophically inclined.
I don't believe in myself.
Am I peculiar?

I have one friend,
550 Grand Street,
Mrs. Botwinck.

I broke a leg in 1948.
I thought I wouldn't recuperate.

I became nervous.
Here are my pills.

These rooms are very airy.
I must have cross ventilation.

5.

Becky Feinman,
you let marriage go,
took a boarder 30 years,
Mr. Kalter,
whose pants folded wool
lie buried on corner chair—
Such big cuffs

6.

I climb the steps of death, Q-Tips
and flies feed on Eternity's menopausal sweat,
Apt. 14 padlocked, Mendel Solomon's left.

7.

Turn of century vines
Furnished room
On an old curb
Morris Klein

I'll see a little sunshine yet
Cheese can't hurt me
They can have all my records

8.

I'm ashamed
That chandelier
used to shine
like gold

My husband
God killed him
We had a restaurant
136 W. 17th St.

Every Wednesday
Collecting for Yeshiva
I gave bottle of milk potatoes
hard-boiled eggs better than my customers

I was glad   They davnd

My niece came
I should forget a few weeks
and go with her
to Chester, N.Y.

That night
I opened the door
What I thought was the bathroom
and fell to the basement

       Since then I'm dizzy dizzy
       dizzy
dumb deaf dizzy I can't catch
the words people say

I cry more than I eat
I need someone to clean my windows

9.

I need money
I owe my phone
Everything is black & white,
Mrs. Sylvia Leon

Burned eye area
You say not how
"Here's the needle"
Diabetes heart trouble
High blood pressure no downs
Infected toe
"You see the puss"

10.

Young man,
in two years
I'll be 70

I'll be 100
and never
a yellow-belly

Three black guys
grabbed my collar
I said, "Listen here"

My Puerto Rican friends
pulled out knives
crossed the street
Told me go inside

I'll machine-gun down
everybody

and put up a sign:
I know what to do

11.

At 12,
they took him to a doctor
He wouldn't open his mouth
Wouldn't eat
At his daughter's wedding
he wouldn't eat
To this day
"No vegetables"
The doctor pulled hairs
from his head
to make him scream

12.

A complaint to the Hotline
    milk ½ gallon 94 cents
    Breyer's ½ gallon $2.19
    Hi-C 20 cents extra
Poor people victimized
at Columbia St. Pioneer

Please throw out
these thick-skinned peaches

13.

Union Hotel
Jacob lives
    If you want to
    find him

go down to OTB
Home at 6

14.

Children scoot problem stoops,
I'm seated in chairs bought 1914,
Networks of synagogues decline;
Opportune Mr. Softee sells permissiveness
And our language finds shrapnel;
Blacks, Whites, Hispanics, Orientals & Others,
Fight vague authorities like deserts,
Living in a war zone
Where we shine our badness to God.
My quick prayer:
Let the lamb lie down on Astor Pl.

15.

Not death the sage
    rising, rising
Face opens deep as age

16.

Wed.

Mike:

You owe Clara a timesheet
for 7/18/22.
Also please complete
last week's outside forms
in your box so I can sign
them.
Thanks.

George.

TO THE RECEPTIONIST

Lilacs, Maggie
Smell, be high
all week, burn,
Buzz, satisfied

Too cloudy
Deeds're a score
Bands cost money
Love remains poor

May, at last
Pace and survive
Friday come fast
Delicious word

GLANCING AT MY LIFE

You feel systematically incorruptible, something
Akin to those emblazoned St. Francis of Assisi postage stamps

Alive to the instant
The unruly young
The old confluent
Nestled in the pliant metropolis
You bespoke an unspoiled child

Not God's existence
Stupidity obsesses the heedless citizen's concerns

You were employed in 1975
During the night assembling breakfasts,
Prince Street, a concessionaire's headquarters
Located dimly in ground floor simple maze

A wino slept there occasionally
Upon an awesome empty table
Under the aproned manager's solitary auspices while I
Packaged buttered onion rolls in wax paper bags

Alas, your formed character precedes movable type
If wakened tomorrow, you won't feel interrupted

You've dreamed richly of the Orient,
Of trained statues, devas
Poised like wooden atoms, of similarity
And white and green, of buried wines

Fastened in dusted carafes, a fluid light,
Trees close by, comradery and expertise,
A dream of privacy

The day tosses awnings crank
All of dawn is automatic
The funnel of wind
Collecting rags over the hoary Nile subsides
Exquisite beasts hitched to buggies mortally jaunt

O star-spangled haiku! O sunless lofts!
Love is unbelievably irrelevant

And it snows in Zurich
Stocked with cognac and furs
The snowflakes, jewels one's heart

Favorably evaluates,
Slash the nothingness and flutter to improve
The lake with kisses

You slowly walk past your favorite building, 1200 Broadway
It's Edwardian yet simple like a shield painted brown
Something handmade
Right on the corner of 29th Street
You feel maneuvered

Remember a swamp appealed
How our mind swayed near the undulating blossom
A desirous landmark seemed to toll
It crouched personifying absence
It looked feathery harsh orchestral
A ground swell action painting like Times Square

Here's the quintessential you,
In a bookstore in old Georgetown, D.C.

Through splendid Versailles you hike,
You feel happy and average . . .

The cobblestones glimmer pitifully
Installed to withstand endless tension
How much twilight routinely dances there
Jitterbugging in the muffled roar
In the wake of inference
An uncontrollable, irrepressible dance
Plummeting and tumbling, invariably transformed

Prodigal, circulating among remarks,
Your encompassed blood
A shadowless idea,
A unit of assertions
Chickens roast glazed with fluorescence

Nonchalant, demeanor bold
A pigeon on wise 14th Street, a bull in Candia, a mouse
Prompt, scheming, mulish
You soar, you continuously rage

WHISPERINGS

Upland and fens
Mist-tufted, cogs

Sprinting soot clings
Enisled to stone

On Cam's edge steadfastly
Controlled punts roll

Happening market stamps apace
Serious intention is engaged

Element clearing skies
And leaves circularly indoors

The slightly foolish beetle
Is in mud and algae
Other than it behaves

One foot hedges
Dahlias' provenance

VIA IMPERIALE

Giovanni, Giovanna,
Rita and Giantonio
Would found a school

Rita says
Money is the problem

Bountiful sunshine warms Manhattan
Last night I dreamed of moment
Empty Yankee Stadium lights
Turned on finalizing renovations

Sara, Michela, Serafina
Two marijuana plants
300 flowers

Via Imperiale, Via Fantasia

No danger
Reborn six-legged spider in bathtub
Share food, drink tea in bowl steaming

> *December 18, 1980*
> *for artist Giovanni d'Agostino and family*
> *Santa Maria Codi Fiume, Ferrara, Italy*

CLINCH

Let's deviate,
That's not frightening,
Alive, voluntarily.

Let's not have acidity,
A pathetic yearning,
Far away—

Inside sings,
Zeus molestation,
Mind rages, still—

Fingers tap
Thighs, crossed
Legs, naturally
Awaiting.

Lovers hate an image,
Go somewhere, silly
Enough, alone.

Poor, in Misery, or
Stay; to broil,
Bring home foil.

Manliness untroubled.

THIRTY-FIVE PENCE

There will be Companionship,
Statement, Felicity;
I thought I'd thought
Of everything.

You carry on.
A man's not drawing
A straight line, he's
Drawing a curved one.

Precious like Certainty
Were composed streets
Where loaded glass towers
Take over the fullness.

Neither is it a thing
Mediated by time.

Filth of cigarettes
And dirt, dirt upsetting.
Marvelous. I equally know
The world is about tomorrow as well.

FRANCES LeFEVRE WALDMAN, ELEGY

What Paradise inscribed

She planted, strove to
Lead, coax, water
Fair months, her radiance

And wrath of moonlight's creek,
And the sanitary odor
In parks, faintly humid

Her happily shrewd,
Direct, moderate ways
Dented me, blessed on earth

May 20, '82

SONNET, AN INTRODUCTION, "BETTER NOT TO THINK"

Young woman in white jeans
Faints, cops kneel to her on platform
No breakfast, severe cramps, weakens
Heat's clutch sprawls, unconscious
You think, train traffic murmurs,
In shambles darkness circulates

New York, when you think
A place forever, sounds dear
Avenues gold strips, rivers
Not merely questions, blunt; halls,
Plentitude, daydreams insistent
Modes, a solemn carnival, peaks,

When you think—clever, chaste,
Old, frail—better not to think

STRIPPED

I see you, woman, girl
Not tomorrow

Instead, very thoughtful
I bring groovy
Unities of the thorn, one
Pink, babble to you, and go

A white one, ditching the articulate

Why, because you are daring
And run on perfect legs,
Do well-wishers feel obligated
To comfort you battling
A clan of aches?

Mist fell
And when the mist continued
She, Buddha, stuck out her tongue, hiding
And we exchanged superficial looks

It is my stranded goal
Like salvaging a patriotic beer's design
Pompons, to sniff
And carved the stems

FUN AND CHANGE

Fun is like an old friendship,
dualism apart.
The rebuilt porches of cozy streets.
A panoramic skyline, many appointments.

*

Change, somehow
is redundant.
Change gets to you.
The miles are alike.

VALENTINE'S

Quick woman, voices
Incidental ride the air

Church sun bathes lavender,
Red brick exposure of rectory
adjacent, diminutive rectangle,
Slender chimney's released smoke

Jerusalem is
a crucial place—
disaster and insistence reign

The food vendor's done,
reattaching axle wheels to
his scoured cart

I marvel
at translucent sky
How you contain beauty

A SPANISH SONG

La Policia! Agua!
Shout Madrid's angels

Heat wave
        black valises
                luminosity
El callejon de toros

Holy tobacco
No water at all morning
Picasso's bird studies
surfaced adroitly in
latter day's windowsill of mansion

Clean, balconied lodgings, coffee
Durables, stabilized
Las Ramblas to the pier night
The impoverished see with internal tears

Fair, serene, El Greco land
Aspirations, grasped gold, red wildflowers

Luminosity!   Scarlet Geraniums!   Machine guns!

Walk tall in Madrid, eloquent
land of lemon trees and frills, O
Men and Women of Intellect

A WEDDING WITH YOU

Like the song's scales,
A few minutes' difference.
Ever my confidence, play-
Ful wife, my adoration.

Luck, summon family, florist.
Unlock the courthouse.
Let no prayer disturb
Seamstress, judge or cook.

Maids, hurry. This is she.
Sun and moon interlace
The whirled dawn. Mothers,
Be calm and proud.

Dry August winds brush Chinese
Lantern Plants (Winter Cherries),
Tap gravity's flesh.
We share your might.

Bride, in day's course
Ours this vowing's distinction.
Stone Abbeys fashion an aggrieved
Europe, hearts' realism chimes.

A WOMAN

"I come to haunt you,"
Pure as doubt, civilized.

I miss home too, all day
The forwarded, bulk resemblances
& elegant spirits
stored in laundry room
foundations, borderline adversaries.

I refer to Idlewild on occasion.
I derive urbanity from the poor sun;
Hands arched, a lush breeze, perhaps of blackberries.
An unbroken look and everything else.

And unrelenting, unforgiving,
Hazard the cartoon ocean's
impulsed grip, in pursuit of contention.
Trails of mist
bewailing protean money's core.
The full moon trampolined. Factored starlight.

The landscape emerged; worshiped clouds
of understanding and factories
whose purposes simplify passionate discourse,
span the elevated horizon.
A woman, loud and defiant like a flower.

UNCLE ISMAEL

died last night.

Young Migdalia thinks
Cousin Freddie in Puerto Rico
telephoned news misinformed.
No one's home in Brooklyn though,
to lend her beautiful idea probability.

The man loved to talk
and eat.

Señor Villegas dreamed clearly
of the dead man after midnight.
Nervous, he lets fall
half a toasted bagel to the floor
and juggles a fork.

Finally, the truth comes.
Feeling ill, Ismael bathed.
Hurry, said Miriam.
We'll rush to the hospital.

I want to go dressed,
said Ismael Falcon.

He passed away spiffy and shoeless.

Can you believe it, said Nellie.
He was a real sharp dresser.

LETTER FROM MARIELLA

You probably feel alienated now
because I never write to anybody
but I respect and think
sweetly of you always

Nellie's husband is beautiful
Maybe I could get into something
if he does have a brother
I want to marry somebody special

I received two honor certificates—
in mathematics and graciousness,
and May 25 had an emotional
prom night with two escorts

Freddie does the bolero,
No salsa or disco,
so I danced those and the former
because I don't waste time

I went to the beach Monday
with Freddie who'd slept over
And how is your husband
whom I adore with an obsession

Please write, tell everyone
Many kisses and strong hugs
and I will visit soon to break the peace
so you can drive me around

BUTTER HILL*

My beloved sky's face
is indescribable.
It sheds reminiscence
upon the vivid world
that enlists
our infatuate sense.

I crawl beneath its most
terrible conference. Right away,
right away. The sun decisively chants.
Mountains gape like scissors.
A piece of the day is formed.

The world spins and envelops the leaves,
Oceans likewise coo. They
shed lost sounds upon the shore.
The risings and fallings of the colored earth
shatter my beloved sky.

*Now called Storm King Mountain, it faces north, protectively overlooking the site of the Continental Army's New Windsor Cantonment in Vails Gate, New York, in Orange County. To the Revolutionary soldiers stationed there in 1782, the assortment of rocks arrayed on the familiar hill exhibited yellowish hues.

LONGER DAYS

for Nellie Villegas

1.

Unsettled, all quiet
No thing dissembled

Ethereal snow
Covers the fabricated
Riverside

Love evoked

Sturdy matrix,
Patient smiler
In the cold format:

Gray, steepled

2.

Overhead,
Voluminous lightning
Rifts the dome.

The blizzard suggests
An ultimate dream.

Shadows drop.

Negotiating such magic
Lifted faces shine.

3.

The Sicilian cobbler
Mr. A. Fontana

Arrived in America
Twenty years ago

His prices are low
For expertly mending

Ladies' and Mens' shoes
Solemn and amicable, he's

Accommodated himself
To our culture

4.

Color fringed
The whitened blend of trees—
Stark intentions, hill and plane;
The ritualistic eye inserts a red dashboard.

Oh clean morning air, asleep!
I fail to transcribe starlight's
Utterances.
　　　　　But I wish, in
Tow of winter's iron, to cultivate
Humankind's molten energy.

Crew downcast.

5.

Dark fire, the face
Faultlessly composed

Sensual like snow
Crowns mountain

Witty, prized
Indomitable mother

Vanity typifies us
Cast in heaven

Small features, a photograph,
High-priestess of Marzipan

6.

Rain set forth,
All rain, upon rosebush
And windshield, rain

So pressed against
The avenue's shops,
A violet gray dye abounds,
In disclosed strokes, washed light . . .

New, bustling day.
Men discuss—
One bearded, one carries a briefcase—
Recommend whatever

Run smoothly, Day
Later, descend

I step into the park
where Spring advances

    blue warbling
        savage carnations
            $1.00 per bunch

The sun is batting
Eighth and hitting .215

Rectangular lawn holds green
Devoid of receded snow

7.

Traffic gropes toward
Newer petals . . .

Tearful duet posted outside
Manufacturers Hanover Trust

Serve up slow
Electric blues,

Mild crosswinds,
An apple suspended in air

Stem intact, coincidence,
Masks a proper gentleman

8. *The Drama*

He is alone by the window
Ya fuckin' dope

Goodbye

Don't leave him
Alone by the window

You got ten seconds to get in
Or I'm leavin'

He's alright
Go on and leave

9.

"Sunshine fills the world
To make you a life"

Walk, back
And forth along
The esplanade, Grandma

Her yoga-tuned memory
Quickens paying homage
To burlap.

10. *Bryant Park*

Few clouds, claiming lightness.
Midday honied river,
Leaping horns.

Even the skeletal woods,
London Plane trees separating
Humble public grounds
From venial skyscrapers
Pipe (allegro molto vivace),
Above love-making revelers,
Brass lances absent summer.

I write tongue-shaped
    words in buds.

Ha! Four winds
Rumble in unison . . .
Completely, specifically.

Bryant Park sizzles.

Esteemed pollution's
Peripheral holocaust
Confronts fashion's mythic
Body language of strangers

And I have mistreated sadly
My own sincere mind.

11. *Esquire*

I see an umbrella out there
So I imagine it's drizzling
The way it was before

No one so thoughtful
And ponderous as you

12. *The Wind*

The wind seeks its home,
Knocks about along roads
Has clarity among rafters

A girl tempts
The round sea's edge

Personal a top
In galoshes walking away
Hear it howl "how" lost

13.

Before school bell rings
Smoke and vulgarity—

Sunday afternoon fog
Bank sweeps office buildings

Business as usual,
Trees will flourish

IN MARCH

Bus routes intertwine
The managed surroundings,
A toxic environment
Allotted trees

Sweet month, convictions,
Cherubic sparrows instruct,
Impervious old folk
Purchase breads

Globe's ethnocentric
Civilities distress,
Laden with trends
And familiarity

Blessings in stride,
In mind to forefend,
Plant critical seeds,
Encourage sentiment

HELLO TO _____

This November breeze
Lifts a sail, the rice paper blind,
A rent-stabilized apartment, course set,
The odd sensation calmly falling

I'd rushed home, typically wearied,
Abreast of what general excitement
In the air (No drumming
On desks), after two hour
Mandatory workshop held weekly
For new inner-city teachers,
And found my building under siege

Silent police closing in
Congregated on the staircase,
Armed experts, indefatigable public eyes
Representing the bulwark of rectitude
ABC camera teams stood by

Testing his flash
A photographer snapped pictures
Of the high-spirited onlookers
Sternly posed el barrio women
Bundled in coats
The eternal darkness a thin backdrop

Havoc-riddled days
I'll hand the dog my undershirt to chew

I could give no help
The coherent energy pleading
Beyond the peephole for cooperation
As, aroused from torments,
He awakened to the terrible appeals

Descending in a chair
Three flights past my door,
A charming man loudly complaining,
"Great . . . don't work so hard,"
To ambulance, a recast Black Maria,
And Bellevue

A ROSE

Singled out,
Plain,
Clearly red

It passes by,
Smiling, old

A stem's
The body

RALPH, THE MONK

About to start a serious fire, I'll
Go home, burn a stick of incense when
It's late, that's a vogue I own up to,
Turn the radio on for a while and quiet down,
A blessing of solitude on the hearth.
I take long trips to the countryside alone,
Where no people are, in other words,
But the inoffensive column of smoke,
Reeking of meditation, chiefly will do.

Man is heartless, whoever
Oppose that, raise suspicious eyebrows,
Declares himself a fool. I laugh
In his face unintelligibly, makes him forget . . .
Just look around you, fine, straight at me,
Into the dawn, if you like, of all this ruin,
When the blue streets are empty,
Except the lost soul or two, a nuisance
For the jobber arranging flowers in buckets
Who's not interested in forgiveness, he won't
Listen to the wind. Work consumes him, there's
No praise attached to his deeds. Maybe he's charmed
Some ladies, finds it clumsy to feel jealousy or rage,
But he's envious of the dead, the hours they keep,
He'd murder with abandon for a parking spot.

You'll notice it's the trick of suspense
That makes customers shout approval; hypnotists
Depend on volunteers. I learned to cakewalk

Across the stage when I was in school. Something
Acrobatic, today's breakdance shoulder spins,
The popular mazurka, makes 'em howl. Minoan
Gymnasts dove headlong on the run, and in midair
Gripped the charging bull's horns, to equate
Life with a somersault, to save their own skins
As the martyrs, for instance St. Christopher, could not.

This neighborhood, I've lived in it
All my life, I sing too loudly, has changed.
I've dreamt of other things, Looked into
Motion Pictures once, played a Zulu
Headhunter, trod stomped dust, wore a straw
Minidress. The stills from that adventure hung
For months next to the ices listed
On the wall behind the pastry shop counter.
I was congratulated, my agent had an outline
And an honest grin. I opened a savings account.
I flew about to meetings showing
My deference to all, and my
Social polish. But as the feathers of opportunity
Were drawn nigh to dangle before me,
I despised the world's lack of taste, and
I was at that point reassured by feeling
Out of touch. I dismantled the scheme,
Auditioning now and then, as other men give
Charity, for a lark. I carry my ten pounds
Of balls around, I'm up before the sun.
The Boys' Club on 10th Street's my alma mater, though

Now it's coed, like a brothel. My popularity's no enterprise.
I'm not easily provoked, or grievanced
For that matter. I make my living
Doing this, standing guard.
I have to take my collar off.

Look, I've seen women, however built, grown straight,
Able to perpetuate their tender vows
Of integrity without being stained by the debris
Of their surroundings like ugly snakes.
Their entertaining wits are Reason's product,
Unequaled by the devoutest prayers.
Women could run the space program with their talk.
My God, the ones I know blab all night.
I have to turn a lamp on when they visit to be polite.
And sure, she was also a fine, fine bitch.
So, I was forced to make a choice, I put
Myself in two scenarios at once,
A life of matrimony or of religion,
Understanding my wishes under a microscope
Were elaborate, available in either framework.
Following my orders is lavishness enough.
I introduced her to my best friend. They tied the knot.
The truth's the truth; I don't mind, I like to hear it.
Whatever your situation is, or your sister's
Someone else I know is marrying soon,
They'll be cosy I hope, a well-dressed pair,
Indebted to Sunday for a stroll,
Smart shoppers. If something's too expensive,
I do without it. The single life's better.
"Live with her? What kind of man
Do you think I am?" he says. "The shoe fits,"
He says. Long as she doesn't split him
In half. "They have rights, too," I said.

California? Well, rest up. Have a swell
Time. An aunt of mine lives there . . .
Santa Monica. Visited her once seven
Years ago who's 86 now. Cooks? Sure,
Does everything. Walks and talks. Funny,
I don't recollect the town whatsoever, just
The type of street it was, telephone wires
And shady trees. Oh yeah, it's on the Coast.
I moved back in with my father later on.
He's very strict, you know. We don't see
Eye to eye. Be asleep by 9 o'clock. Moves
Safes for a living. Remarried. "But," he said,
"There's the 'frigerator." You have your own bedroom."
Looked for a place to rent, in a renovated building.
I wanted to give the landlord a beating . . .
2 months deposit . . . Wasn't even Jewish, an Arab.
$850 a month. He smiled, well.
I'd lived with a friend's grandmother,
Took care. She died. A day that some
Look forward to. She welcomed it.

The nice, the not so nice,
I'm going to buy a picture of myself,
Give everyone a copy to place on a dresser,
You can see my face, first thing in the morning.
You got problems, contact my lawyer.
Here comes Wilfred, late as pleased, gifted,
Shy, especially independent, not the interfering
Type. Long hair, thick glasses, a razor blade.
He gets picked on. "No moleste, no moleste."
Hey, I'll talk to you, I'd better go.

THINKING

The poem is a dream
Your frame youthful
A sculpture living

Soft as flannel
Solid as rock

Your backside
Leaning
Blue-collar
Against kitchen table

The subject's Poetry
Riding the crest
Paper-thin
Snowflake

The thought in my head
To speak with you
The room happily making sense

PUBLIC SPEAKING

I know the thoughts
That go through a man's mind
I'll write a book about it one day

BEAUTIFUL MORNING

for Jim Brodey

Beautiful morning
Entered on tide charts

Vast café's mopped floors
Serenity 'midst ordered silverware

Rip, leafless bounty of
Drifts untrod,
Branches which thwart
The unmarked sky

& dawn's ripened
Like the sunken
Turkish coffee bean
Toward bitterness

Vagrant breaths,
Guarded, fleeting, useless
Beautiful damnation

Rustled newspaper startles
Frozen to sidewalk in ice
Soft my footsteps
Quiet wind

Stars in rigid orbit
Seem to flicker and expand

Influencing mind
And heart tangibly
Across immense distance

WINTERTIME

1.

The trees enthroned
Like destinies

Housing motionless
In foreground

I walk in judgment
Listen to skies dance

2.

Planted strides
Long streets fashionable
Sing these droves
Ancient matter
At length the skull

Looks of contradiction
My lustful essence
Giant cities, recombined Chaos,
Like a transparent icing

3.

Afternoon darkness
Begins

Inside, here
Grandma's reddish
Bookcase
The dust particles
Reformulate in clusters

An immobile will somehow
Of snow has fallen
Suspended on branches and clothesline

FILIUS ANTE PATREM

He wore no hat
in summer
or in winter blasts

A bald spot
certainly
couldn't matter less

He smirked
How quickly I'd grown
He said I was rough

I contradicted much
Agreed but
to the time of day

So seeing the light
Respecting my airs
He said I was tough

Years have flown
I welcome always
his ghost to stay

He'd blue eyes,
an optimistic atheist
And Jesus Christ was black

HER MUSE

She's thrilled to explicate.
She is better than the soil.

In her evolved opinion
Daylight's a convenient dissonance
Like a horse made of water.
Her excesses resonate depth
Like actual wild swans of equilibrium

Volatile, wholesome, impeccable—
The cruel ocean strengthens her visage.
Her quiddities convene.
Nothing else is too definite.
Delight fades. She sees her companions
The trees and the sky.
The planet's core is transitory.

Universe capable of medicine,
She structures the precepts. Dispersed
Lines, of necessity, locate highways.
Her advice: "Do what you want."
After reflection, in the ponderous rays,
Her excited eyes condition truths.

ADVICE

Come down
Go further

HIGHLIGHT

Glaciers reaped,
A lover's notion,
The rock-stunned
Shoreline.

I survive my happiness.
Your insight is ever true.

The wind ascends,
Pivots, caresses.
Aware, indigenous,
Mild among pines.

I survive my happiness.
Your insight is ever true.

The road winds.
A car penetrates the mist
In a drastic, too
subtle world.

We race the clock;
Intensity, repose.
I survive my happiness.
Your insight is ever true.

LOOKING BACK

Elsewhere, rocketing sleep plumbed,
Night's abruptly savored,
The shipwrecked moon's like a pearly gauze,
Concerns, day's uses, escalate

Hoboes leap cheerily, corners trapped, squeezed
Out of buildings, exhilarated, some makeshift game—
Bicycle inner tube,
Parking regulation sign a peg—
Frayed, disenfranchised, beauty missed,
Their grog-sodden zest
Argues contrarily in domesticity's favor,
Something to eat, an egg?

Kin, motivated cousins, myself irritable,
Declines presentiment, more right
Than wrong, not fortuitously ruled,
Basic, ineluctable haste

And your mouth compressed of shining roses,
Your body luscious, milk and powdered chocolate,
And by your instincts emancipated,
You reminisce, your habits bloomed

TO LEX ROMAINE, A FOLKSINGER

Your fame existed
clear across the tracks
to Public Square,
and continues thereabouts
outside Pocono resorts
and Gus Genetti's smorgasbord

In 1970
Nixon's forces reached Cambodia
You'd sing half the night
in a bar on North Franklin Street
for drinks and pocket money

I remember your style
No anger, no mockery

As hunters know the forest,
each vertiginous bend and glade,
you cradled the guitar greedily
You always played
Arlo Guthrie's hit "City of New Orleans"

Hotel Sterling's granite crucifix
regal lit west
above the eastern riverbank
of blue-blooded brick estates
We spoke inconsequentially,
but you were an imposing figure

EIGHT SONNETS

You cannot yet buy one dish of Chinese food in all Italy.

—Ezra Pound, "Canto LXXX"

I.

Arrange it thusly use this phrase,
Infer no season, nor whereabouts,
& remember this, you chose no precedent,
Had no plan to rob Tampax and Coppertone,
Those batteries weren't in stock & you waltzed
Past the guard, almost affronted, discombobulated,
As the humorous wind folds and overturns
Vacant lawn chairs on the roof, as now
You stand desirous by the pool's edge;
Truth's a battered garbage can, lid's askew;
Infinitely particular but for itself regarded;
Coat it with sweetness yet don't attenuate;
What's mine is mine; besides, plum-colored delirium,
Life's too short, you'll just do your part until it's done.

II.

The calm part of your brain,
Puppeteer, diplomat, clown,
Vigilant prospector after gists, fads &
Answers in earnestness readies to dissuade
Intrusive death, the know-nothing, desperate lout,
But whose odds stand defined, opinion right,
What over pause, contingency, or doubt's good
You can't point-blankly study through, one shouldn't
Assure unless risk pomposity, flamboyance, abstract
Passion, and who dies for tomorrow in civilized culture
Amiss, divorced from Art's vision,
Discriminations unexpressed, media hype the unmanned cart?
Yet do thoughts bend sinewy, tomatoes
Cherish the vine, intuit the destined sandwich.

III.

Memory that delivers palpable thoughts,
Truly an abstract thing; treats of cuisine,
Romance tasted with effect and relished;
Sensation has a context which settles inside;
The gratification flees with the distinctive hour,
Nuance cannot recapture the day. Yet memory traveled
Will approach the results, conversation brought to a close,
Board the earlier train, see time's point
When your knowledge was less, your painted mood blacker,
Adamantly wished tests, though now, sweetest thought,
Play in summer just as hot, reddened millions
Shade the beach, divested of fury, tacitly confidential
(Meager regulations), like shocked witnesses midtown
Ham N' Eggs franchise, circa 1960, waiter headwhipped in brawl.

IV.

Squibs, flowering suns, doubleheader balloons,
Black market the size of a large closet
Essentially, on Mott St., Carmine St., it's declassified
For the good it will do death on the check-out lines,
And I stepped on a used needle, got anxious and high,
Couldn't believe the deeds of the street
Happening to me, where newcomers to town
Soiled their shirts for upholstery, aside undisturbed,
Deprived but independent, in need of sleep,
While the air cooled, my knowledge had gone into it;
Hopeful mind of tragic implications followed
By a sense of depravity because thought eats action,
Why get up in the morning, resolution of a crisis,
Warnings at the door, snaky comprehension, awfulness?

V.

Don't stand accused by a generality,
Woman, developed thoughts marry grace
In your able brain, frank and meticulous
Charms; your consideration's no dream.
The gilded numbers change, not the incomprehensible
Digits. Surrender to the milky galaxy of years.
& Lord, circulate the words like money till it hurts, I'll
Draw attention to the misused farmer's plight,
And make each letter count. Happy Birthday, Independence.
Dates, dues, occasions, personality within earshot.
A stubborn malediction to define thee,
Utmost precious one, while paramedic's van's
Headlight's coincident with skunk's promenade, ho!,
Altered the steak house lounge ambience.

VI.

You mask impatience well,
Adhering to expectations past confinement,
Accent on fact, swift praising merits, the word
Righteous fits, though like our passing time
Which shuns debate, midnight obtains an admirer.
Long may fortune serve you hazards of perfection,
Shared sun, loved moon, complimented stars and starlets,
A cast's narcissistic energy's plastic unification.
And boldly our glassy lights point, thread nervous aether
Which supersedes consciousness like a robust grape;
Conciliatory persistence stuns and stirs
New attitudes with a serviceable beat, a few props
Transforming dawn's web of predictions, indifferent bricks,
All there is, nothing to lean on save the lesson and script.

VII.

Drought, plague, old instruments,
Leaked plutonium baths, chased sunsets,
Hard finding a shirt I wanted, Macy's floor
Walked expending a sense of difficulty,
Cottons tuned, knits valued, pointless
To mention it, no problem mentioned slightly,
Or make worry yours an issue worth;
Developers of mineral rights keep yokels astute,
Spare change nothing to sneeze at, lavender, crystal,
Wealthy Dionysus torn apart in the jungle.
But assume a discourse as between men and ideas,
Like gentle ancestry in an opulent Paradise.
Eileen, everyone's got a straight face; track it,
Kicked back, watching paid TV in a suffering land.

VIII.

Dove come hidden to rest, 18 hrs.,
Its disjointed neck a distressful matter, was odd
Attraction closer to home than thunder jamming
Foibles, claims, contacts, dividends, snaring
Finicky pursuit, where separate buildings'
Connect formed air's passage, ladder of slate,
Window ledge, day long, and a little magic's noticed.
Sonia's gifts from Kenya, mask of woman in wood,
Nailed through braid-loop diadem to wall, and coffee beans
I had ground extra fine by Mrs. Shim, Sue, Jason's wife,
At DiBella's European Deli (Inc.), thank you again,
In my time of this calculated evening, as under protection,
Their distracted elders clapping festive, ecstatic offspring prostrate
Strike rain's curbed flow, for cool respite, and to squirm.

OLD RESOLVE

That golden beauty appointed youth—
Time's no coin to keep

But look! A magic beaming glass
To look on dawns
Of no apparent note,
Trumpet peals of grief

Pursued disdain my emphasis
With language to distort my strife
Accursed like a foolish thief
With solitude my bride

My heart sees how it, forlorn,
No decline of grace opposed
I mocked symmetrical life and death
I'd live with keener sense

BAD FEELINGS

It was as though
I'd exited hell and slipped
Oh, well

True to none,
She simplified
Beauty's magnitude,
Bent properly
On wry assessment,
Her wretchedness
An earnest afterthought

Once, winter sparked
Those flattering eyes;
We'd stepped to bed, I
Can't remember what I said,
Her laughter rang thin air

Heads turned,
I saw the crowd's merriment,
Our private grins scrutinized

TO A CERTAIN MR. RICHARD ALBERT, MY LANDLORD

You're a man looks afraid to sleep
May you never rest in gladness
May you never enjoy a spring scent,
Life's colors, a sky inexplicably real!
May you never enjoy life!
May your food of the marketplace taint
Or spoiled in preparation be

In humped obeisance 'fore hooves of the Golden Calf of ruin,
May your capacity to understand emotions
Dwindle to a flea's and convulse your nerves' bounty
May you never take a second to breathe deeply

And talk about repairs!
Do something about that wife!
Buy the right gift, make her smile
She hasn't my dog's politeness
May you and the missus both stink awfully bad,
Like defiled rooms, as you age forgetting to wash
Watch out, on your crooked road of lies!
Cruel, no place hereafter
Your menacing of the effulgent void, pipsqueak,
Makes shabby your every gesture

Die without water for abusive thirst!
Where's the flame to treat your possession?
Spurned by martyrs, licking your ears demons' torments,
Fall to hell via uninspected elevator shaft,
Wearing your piece-of-shit raincoat

POEM

So to sing for myself
My concerns
Man, myself
Night commencing

No deeds to calculate
Than discernments
Man's like the hard sea
The sea yielding songs

So I am drawing myself without excess
The root of my exertions
The paramount center
Unswerving

I taste in myself
My singing's cause
The meditative sea
The flower's affirmation

My heart maintains no aura
My heart amassed of particles
My heart a sober witness
My heart a tower of song

A LADY'S HEARTACHE

Snow builds quietly, antithetical;
Lamplight glows 100 watts inside a borrowed room;
The lemon tea set to cool,
She writes preoccupied,
          page after spiral-bound page:
"The evening inclines to statement, a memory,
Boots dry on newspaper mats, snowy hours
          brush the windowpanes . . .
Indecision makes us false . . .
I wish for no malice to linger.
Your ways generous, I stood
          before the mirror weak and emboldened . . .
Tomorrow films of spray harass the driver in pursuit . . .
Best to plead no rendezvous
          nor demonstrate affection over the phone.
This action is wise.
Our venture culminates without further plans."

ERNIE

A devoted seminary student,
You declined without reproof
The countenancing mantle of priesthood.
A marine biologist, unburdened
By class, inspired in Mayagüez
By phosphorescent molecules,
The dark waters' terrible power
To regenerate and corrode,
Nothing cooled your promise. You
Bought your folks a home:
They never saw any bills.
Your spirit was tolerant,
A generous and contented one.
Your will specified a funeral
In the Bronx, at Ortiz's
Since your parents don't drive.
They were spared a hassle
Commuting to Manhattan. And you
To an underlit world,
Escorted under no duress,
Lifted out of sedation,
Your ghost like a deep kiss,
Perhaps you hear the bereaved reminisce.
Your sister said to Mark,
"Everybody he met
Fell in love with him."
"I did," Mark said.

Thirty-nine, soon and successful,
Emptied of suffering, removed from sadness,
Wickedness, jealousy, disease.
Life not enjoyed
To the utmost is a sin.

EARTH TO LANGSTON

Casual Harlem
In the morning
Hot September day
And you wonder why
The fuss race and race

Wise lady, reading
At a bus stop
Not looking up
Old, bony,
Uncommon, statuesque

Boulevards of worship
Red Rooster Tavern
Nailed real shut
Condominiums 110th
The black nation's home

A DAUGHTER

Be above worldly attainments;
Concentrate like plants and stones
But seek fun.

Passing between extremes,
All that's right formed her;
Indisputably mysterious platelets,
Her bitterly frowning, lazily smiling face.
Room 925, Miss Muckamuck,
She grew inside a cloud.

Stalks of iris, lily's prime bell,
Flank a dozen crowning roses;
Blue, white, and red aspirations
Tinged by desire,
Her mind's unquenchable tool.

Seventh Avenue: half-crystalized rain
Angles in descent airily.
A harp, long life, heights of love.

And the midwife sat to paperwork.
Gathered under the Village Vanguard awning,
A bunch of enthusiasts to hear Max Roach preside.

AMAZING HAIKU

After the rain
The sweet air tumbled
Like a parade of steam
Outside my window

Wife's feet raised
On bare pillow on folding chair
Reading *Dharma Bums*
A pot of silly yellow mums

I served coffee
And worried with indifference
About old age and survival
That's Bud Powell's music

SHE'S LEAVING HOME

Nervousness obey like an obligation,
Forethought duels the status quo; indigestible
Poisons rise onerously moistening the tongue,
Rain's prepared a taste of metal

Hunger beginning, heaviness strange,
Surmounts the bookish drive to impose
A design like heaven over the candidate's trail, where
Long the chaste spiritual flame dreaded inadequacy

Even a woman's dejection
Discounted inhospitable, society so backward
We recoil from building,
Instead of penitentiaries,
A celestial land of absorbed participants

Oh, shrewd populace, buzzards
Conspiring in abeyance to recognize the misfit,
Whom
If not the homeless outcasts—
Mired in drivel of accusations, lamentably a cappella?

Frivolous sacrifice and bought wealth's
Implausible ennoblements
Desire stirs her to abhor,
A burden once matriculated to remake life

Tangled quiescence parents tethered,
A summer night's chill wind, a dullness draining in blood

TO ELIZABETH

Beth, sweet fish
There, a beginning
Invincible spring
A lonely cry

There, a beginning
Intelligible light
A lonely cry
Infinite, tense

Floods of light
Turn fierce ground
Remorseless, tense
Welcoming eyes

Turn fierce ground
Invincible spring
Intelligent eyes
Beth, sweet fish

praise for *CLINCH*

It is wonderful to have at last this selection of Michael Scholnick's poetry, beautifully edited by his good friends and fellow poets. I have long been an admirer of Scholnick's poetry, both for the twist and dash and bash of its language and for its largeness of mind and bigness of heart. Scholnick had the mysterious ability to be simultaneously dreamy and wide awake in his work. His poetry is filled with the gorgeous luminosity of words in their prime state, words the reader seems to be discovering, alongside the author, for the very first time. And it's rare and inspiring when one poet can be funny both about the universe and his landlord! This book takes me back to the same thrill and lift I felt in first reading Guillaume Apollinaire and Edwin Denby—a healthy rearrangement of sensibility. As Scholnick himself put it: "Let the ancient cortex dismount."

—Ron Padgett

His selected poems represent fifteen years of dazzling work—poems alternately rich, sinewy, chiding, dense, Yiddish, and sexy. . . . I envy the new readers of these oddly declamatory poems of turgidity and sweetness.

—Eileen Myles

about the author

Michael Scholnick (1953–90) was born in Queens, N.Y., and grew up there and in the Bronx. From 1977 to 1986 he coedited the literary magazine *Mag City*. His first chapbook of poems, *Perfume,* was published in 1978, and his second, *Beyond Venus,* in 1980. This book is the first major collection of his poems.

photo by Michael Kellner, 1980